my childcare
RECIPES

ALL THEIR FAVORITES
& MY NOTES

My Details

Name
....

Family Name
....

Phone Number
....

Adress
....
....
....
....

Facebook
....

Phone Number
....

Caution:
in case you find this notebook please contact me with my details above.

Cooking is about passion so it may look slightly temperamental in a way that it is too assertive to the naked eye

Gordon Ramsay

 Notes

If you are a chef no matter how good a chef you are it is not good cooking for yourself the joy is in cooking for others it is the same with music

will.i.am

Type: Starters - Maincourse - Sides&Salades
Dessert

Contents

Page N°	Type	Recipe Name	Created By

Contents

Type: Starters - Maincourse - Sides&Salades
Dessert

Page N°	Type	Recipe Name	Created By

Type: Starters - Maincourse - Sides&Salades
Dessert

Contents

Page N°	Type	Recipe Name	Created By

Notes

What's Cooking This Week!

What to Cook

B: Breakfast - **L:** Lunch - **D:** Dessert

Sat

B ....
L ....
D ....

Sun

B ....
L ....
D ....

Mon

B ....
L ....
D ....

Tue

B ....
L ....
D ....

Wed

B ....
L ....
D ....

Thu

B ....
L ....
D ....

Fri

B ....
L ....
D ....

B: Breakfast - **L:** Lunch - **D:** Dessert

Sat
B ....
L ....
D ....

Sun
B ....
L ....
D ....

Mon
B ....
L ....
D ....

Tue
B ....
L ....
D ....

Wed
B ....
L ....
D ....

Thu
B ....
L ....
D ....

Fri
B ....
L ....
D ....

What to Cook

Sat
B ....
L ....
D ....

Sun
B ....
L ....
D ....

Mon
B ....
L ....
D ....

Tue
B ....
L ....
D ....

Wed
B ....
L ....
D ....

Thu
B ....
L ....
D ....

Fri
B ....
L ....
D ....

B: Breakfast - **L:** Lunch - **D:** Dessert

Sat
B
L
D

Sun
B
L
D

Mon
B
L
D

Tue
B
L
D

Wed
B
L
D

Thu
B
L
D

Fri
B
L
D

15

What to Cook

Sat
B ....
L ....
D ....

Sun
B ....
L ....
D ....

Mon
B ....
L ....
D ....

Tue
B ....
L ....
D ....

Wed
B ....
L ....
D ....

Thu
B ....
L ....
D ....

Fri
B ....
L ....
D ....

B: Breakfast - **L:** Lunch - **D:** Dessert

Sat
B ....
L ....
D ....

Sun
B ....
L ....
D ....

Mon
B ....
L ....
D ....

Tue
B ....
L ....
D ....

Wed
B ....
L ....
D ....

Thu
B ....
L ....
D ....

Fri
B ....
L ....
D ....

17

What to Cook

B: Breakfast - **L:** Lunch - **D:** Dessert

Sat
B ....
L ....
D ....

Sun
B ....
L ....
D ....

Mon
B ....
L ....
D ....

Tue
B ....
L ....
D ....

Wed
B ....
L ....
D ....

Thu
B ....
L ....
D ....

Fri
B ....
L ....
D ....

18

B: Breakfast - **L:** Lunch - **D:** Dessert

Sat
B ....
L ....
D ....

Sun
B ....
L ....
D ....

Mon
B ....
L ....
D ....

Tue
B ....
L ....
D ....

Wed
B ....
L ....
D ....

Thu
B ....
L ....
D ....

Fri
B ....
L ....
D ....

What to Cook

Sat
B ....
L ....
D ....

Sun
B ....
L ....
D ....

Mon
B ....
L ....
D ....

Tue
B ....
L ....
D ....

Wed
B ....
L ....
D ....

Thu
B ....
L ....
D ....

Fri
B ....
L ....
D ....

B: Breakfast - **L:** Lunch - **D:** Dessert

Sat
B ....
L ....
D ....

Sun
B ....
L ....
D ....

Mon
B ....
L ....
D ....

Tue
B ....
L ....
D ....

Wed
B ....
L ....
D ....

Thu
B ....
L ....
D ....

Fri
B ....
L ....
D ....

What to Cook

B: Breakfast - **L:** Lunch - **D:** Dessert

Sat
B ....
L ....
D ....

Sun
B ....
L ....
D ....

Mon
B ....
L ....
D ....

Tue
B ....
L ....
D ....

Wed
B ....
L ....
D ....

Thu
B ....
L ....
D ....

Fri
B ....
L ....
D ....

B: Breakfast - **L:** Lunch - **D:** Dessert

Sat
B ....
L ....
D ....

Sun
B ....
L ....
D ....

Mon
B ....
L ....
D ....

Tue
B ....
L ....
D ....

Wed
B ....
L ....
D ....

Thu
B ....
L ....
D ....

Fri
B ....
L ....
D ....

So if I am cooking I will be steaming vegetables making some nice salad that kind of stuff

Paul McCartney

Welcome the The Cooking Journey

YumYum Recipe

Name ....

From the kitchen of ....

Preparation Time: .... Cooking Time: ....

Ingredients

- ○ ....
- ○ ....
- ○ ....
- ○ ....
- ○ ....
- ○ ....
- ○ ....
- ○ ....
- ○ ....
- ○ ....

Directions

- ○ ....
- ....
- ....
- ....
- ....
- ....
- ....
- ....
- ....
- ....
- ....
- ....
- ....
- ....
- ....
- ....
- ....

MAIN INGREDIENT

SEASONAL VARIATION

DIFFICULTY
- [ ] EASY
- [ ] MEDIUM
- [ ] HARD

COOKING TEMPERA-TUR

TOOLS TO USE

SERVES

DRINK PAIRING

Memories

Date First Tried .... Date First Made ....

This is .... 's Favorite

▶ Made On

o ....
o ....
o ....
o ....
o ....
o ....
o ....

▶ Occasion

o ....
o ....
o ....
o ....
o ....
o ....
o ....

Notes

27

YamYam Recipe

Date ___ / ___ / 20 ___ DAY: . . . .

Name : . . . .

From the kitchen of : . . . .

Preparation Time : . . . . Cooking Time : . . . .

Ingredients

- o . . . .
- o . . . .
- o . . . .
- o . . . .
- o . . . .

- o . . . .
- o . . . .
- o . . . .
- o . . . .
- o . . . .

Directions

- o . . . .
. . . .
. . . .
. . . .
. . . .
. . . .
. . . .
. . . .
. . . .
. . . .
. . . .
. . . .
. . . .
. . . .

MAIN INGREDIENT

SEASONAL VARIATION

DIFFICULTY
- [ ] EASY
- [ ] MEDIUM
- [ ] HARD

COOKING TEMPERA-TUR

TOOLS TO USE

SERVES

DRINK PAIRING

28

Memories

Date First Tried :............: Date First Made :............:

This is :......................................: 's Favorite

▶ Made On

▶ Occasion

- o ....
- o ....
- o ....
- o ....
- o ....
- o ....
- o ....

 Notes

29

YamYam Recipe

Date ___ / ___ / 20 ___ DAY: . . . .

Name : ....

From the kitchen of : ....

Preparation Time: .... Cooking Time: ....

Ingredients

o . . . .   o . . . .

o . . . .   o . . . .

o . . . .   o . . . .

o . . . .   o . . . .

o . . . .   o . . . .

Directions

o . . . .

. . . .

. . . .

. . . .

. . . .

. . . .

. . . .

. . . .

. . . .

. . . .

. . . .

. . . .

. . . .

. . . .

. . . .

MAIN INGREDIENT

SEASONAL VARIATION

DIFFICULTY

- [ ] EASY
- [ ] MEDIUM
- [ ] HARD

COOKING TEMPERATUR

TOOLS TO USE

SERVES

DRINK PAIRING

30

Memories

Date First Tried: .... Date First Made : ....

This is : .... 's Favorite

▶ Made On   ▶ Occasion

○ ....   ○ ....
○ ....   ○ ....
○ ....   ○ ....
○ ....   ○ ....
○ ....   ○ ....
○ ....   ○ ....
○ ....   ○ ....

 Notes

YamYam Recipe

Date ___ / ___ / 20 ___ DAY: . . . .

Name: ....

From the kitchen of: ....

Preparation Time: .... Cooking Time: ....

Ingredients

○ ....   ○ ....
○ ....   ○ ....
○ ....   ○ ....
○ ....   ○ ....
○ ....   ○ ....

Directions

○ ....
....
....
....
....
....
....
....
....
....
....
....
....
....
....
....

MAIN INGREDIENT

SEASONAL VARIATION

DIFFICULTY
☐ EASY
☐ MEDIUM
☐ HARD

COOKING TEMPERA-TUR

TOOLS TO USE

SERVES

DRINK PAIRING

32

Memories

Date First Tried :.............:   Date First Made :.............:

This is :..: 's Favorite

▶ Made On   ▶ Occasion

- ○ ....
- ○ ....
- ○ ....
- ○ ....
- ○ ....
- ○ ....
- ○ ....

 Notes

YumYum Recipe

Date ___ / ___ / 20 ___   DAY: . . . .

Name ....

From the kitchen of ....

Preparation Time: ....   Cooking Time: ....

Ingredients

○ .... ○ ....
○ .... ○ ....
○ .... ○ ....
○ .... ○ ....
○ .... ○ ....

Directions

○ ....
....
....
....
....
....
....
....
....
....
....
....
....
....
....
....

MAIN INGREDIENT

SEASONAL VARIATION

DIFFICULTY
- [ ] EASY
- [ ] MEDIUM
- [ ] HARD

COOKING TEMPERA-TUR

TOOLS TO USE

SERVES

DRINK PAIRING

♥ Memories

Date First Tried: .... Date First Made: ....

This is: .... 's Favorite

▶ Made On   ▶ Occasion

○ ....   ○ ....
○ ....   ○ ....
○ ....   ○ ....
○ ....   ○ ....
○ ....   ○ ....
○ ....   ○ ....
○ ....   ○ ....

 Notes

35

YamYam Recipe

Date ___ / ___ / 20 ___ DAY: . . . .

Name : ....

From the kitchen of : ....

Preparation Time : .... Cooking Time : ....

Ingredients

- ○ ....
- ○ ....
- ○ ....
- ○ ....
- ○ ....

- ○ ....
- ○ ....
- ○ ....
- ○ ....
- ○ ....

Directions

- ○ ....
....
....
....
....
....
....
....
....
....
....
....
....
....
....

MAIN INGREDIENT

SEASONAL VARIATION

DIFFICULTY
- [ ] EASY
- [ ] MEDIUM
- [ ] HARD

COOKING TEMPERATUR

TOOLS TO USE

SERVES

DRINK PAIRING

♥ Memories

Date First Tried: .... Date First Made ....

This is: .... 's Favorite

♥ • ♥ • ♥ • ♥ • ♥ • ♥ • ♥ • ♥ • ♥ • ♥ • ♥ • ♥ • ♥ • ♥ • ♥

▶ Made On

▶ Occasion

○ ....
○ ....

○ ....
○ ....

○ ....
○ ....

○ ....
○ ....

○ ....
○ ....

○ ....
○ ....

○ ....
○ ....

♥ • ♥ • ♥ • ♥ • ♥ • ♥ • ♥ • ♥ • ♥ • ♥ • ♥ • ♥ • ♥ • ♥ • ♥

 Notes

YumYum Recipe

Date ___ / ___ / 20 ___ DAY: . . . .

Name ....

From the kitchen of ....

Preparation Time: .... Cooking Time: ....

Ingredients

o ....   o ....
o ....   o ....
o ....   o ....
o ....   o ....
o ....   o ....

Directions

o ....
....
....
....
....
....
....
....
....
....
....
....
....
....
....
....
....

MAIN INGREDIENT

SEASONAL VARIATION

DIFFICULTY
EASY
MEDIUM
HARD

COOKING TEMPERA-TUR

TOOLS TO USE

SERVES

DRINK PAIRING

38

Memories

Date First Tried: .... Date First Made ....

This is: .... 's Favorite

▶ Made On   ▶ Occasion

○ ....   ○ ....
○ ....   ○ ....
○ ....   ○ ....
○ ....   ○ ....
○ ....   ○ ....
○ ....   ○ ....
○ ....   ○ ....

 Notes

YamYam Recipe

Date ___ / ___ / 20 ___ DAY: . . . .

Name : ....

From the kitchen of : ....

Preparation Time: .... Cooking Time: ....

Ingredients

o .... o ....
o .... o ....
o .... o ....
o .... o ....
o .... o ....

Directions

o ....
....
....
....
....
....
....
....
....
....
....
....
....
....
....
....
....
....
....

MAIN INGREDIENT

SEASONAL VARIATION

DIFFICULTY
[ ] EASY
[ ] MEDIUM
[ ] HARD

COOKING TEMPERA-TUR

TOOLS TO USE

SERVES

DRINK PAIRING

40

Memories

Date First Tried .... Date First Made ....

This is .... 's Favorite

▶ Made On

- ○ ....
- ○ ....
- ○ ....
- ○ ....
- ○ ....
- ○ ....
- ○ ....

▶ Occasion

- ○ ....
- ○ ....
- ○ ....
- ○ ....
- ○ ....
- ○ ....
- ○ ....

 Notes

YamYam Recipe

Date ___ / ___ / 20 ___ DAY: . . . .

Name ....

From the kitchen of ....

Preparation Time .... Cooking Time ....

Ingredients

- ○ ....
- ○ ....
- ○ ....
- ○ ....
- ○ ....

- ○ ....
- ○ ....
- ○ ....
- ○ ....
- ○ ....

Directions

○ ....
....
....
....
....
....
....
....
....
....
....
....
....
....
....
....
....
....
....
....

MAIN INGREDIENT

SEASONAL VARIATION

DIFFICULTY
- ☐ EASY
- ☐ MEDIUM
- ☐ HARD

COOKING TEMPERATUR

TOOLS TO USE

SERVES

DRINK PAIRING

Memories

Date First Tried :............... Date First Made :...............

This is :.................................... 's Favorite

▶ Made On

○ ....
○ ....
○ ....
○ ....
○ ....
○ ....
○ ....

▶ Occasion

○ ....
○ ....
○ ....
○ ....
○ ....
○ ....
○ ....

 Notes

YamYam Recipe

Date ___ / ___ / 20 ___ DAY: . . . .

Name :...:

From the kitchen of :..:

Preparation Time :............: Cooking Time :............:

Ingredients

o . . . .   o . . . .

o . . . .   o . . . .

o . . . .   o . . . .

o . . . .   o . . . .

o . . . .   o . . . .

Directions

o . . . .

. . . .

. . . .

. . . .

. . . .

. . . .

. . . .

. . . .

. . . .

. . . .

. . . .

. . . .

. . . .

. . . .

. . . .

MAIN INGREDIENT

SEASONAL VARIATION

DIFFICULTY
- [ ] EASY
- [ ] MEDIUM
- [ ] HARD

COOKING TEMPERA-TUR

TOOLS TO USE

SERVES

DRINK PAIRING

44

Memories

Date First Tried: .... Date First Made: ....

This is: .... 's Favorite

▶ Made On   ▶ Occasion

○ ....   ○ ....
○ ....   ○ ....
○ ....   ○ ....
○ ....   ○ ....
○ ....   ○ ....
○ ....   ○ ....
○ ....   ○ ....

 Notes

45

YamYam Recipe

Date ___ / ___ / 20 ___ DAY: . . . .

Name : ....

From the kitchen of : ....

Preparation Time : .... Cooking Time : ....

Ingredients

- ○ ....
- ○ ....
- ○ ....
- ○ ....
- ○ ....

- ○ ....
- ○ ....
- ○ ....
- ○ ....
- ○ ....

Directions

- ○ ....
....
....
....
....
....
....
....
....
....
....
....
....
....
....
....

MAIN INGREDIENT

SEASONAL VARIATION

DIFFICULTY
- ☐ EASY
- ☐ MEDIUM
- ☐ HARD

COOKING TEMPERA-TUR

TOOLS TO USE

SERVES

DRINK PAIRING

Memories

Date First Tried :.............: Date First Made :.............:

This is :..: 's Favorite

▶ Made On ▶ Occasion

○ .... ○ ....
○ .... ○ ....
○ .... ○ ....
○ .... ○ ....
○ .... ○ ....
○ .... ○ ....
○ .... ○ ....

 Notes

YamYam Recipe

Date ___ / ___ / 20 ___ DAY: . . . .

Name ....

From the kitchen of ....

Preparation Time: .... Cooking Time: ....

Ingredients

- ○ ....
- ○ ....
- ○ ....
- ○ ....
- ○ ....

- ○ ....
- ○ ....
- ○ ....
- ○ ....
- ○ ....

Directions

- ○ ....
....
....
....
....
....
....
....
....
....
....
....
....
....
....
....
....
....
....
....

MAIN INGREDIENT

SEASONAL VARIATION

DIFFICULTY
- [ ] EASY
- [ ] MEDIUM
- [ ] HARD

COOKING TEMPERA-TUR

TOOLS TO USE

SERVES

DRINK PAIRING

48

Memories

Date First Tried: .... Date First Made: ....

This is: ....'s Favorite

▶ Made On

▶ Occasion

- o ....
- o ....
- o ....
- o ....
- o ....
- o ....
- o ....

 Notes

YamYam Recipe

Date ___ / ___ / 20 ___ DAY: . . . .

Name :...

From the kitchen of :...

Preparation Time :............. Cooking Time :.............

Ingredients

o . . . .   o . . . .
o . . . .   o . . . .
o . . . .   o . . . .
o . . . .   o . . . .
o . . . .   o . . . .

Directions

o . . . .
. . . .
. . . .
. . . .
. . . .
. . . .
. . . .
. . . .
. . . .
. . . .
. . . .
. . . .
. . . .
. . . .
. . . .
. . . .

MAIN INGREDIENT

SEASONAL VARIATION

DIFFICULTY
- [ ] EASY
- [ ] MEDIUM
- [ ] HARD

COOKING TEMPERA-TUR

TOOLS TO USE

SERVES

DRINK PAIRING

50

♥ Memories

Date First Tried :............... Date First Made :...............

This is :...: 's Favorite

♥ • ♥ • ♥ • ♥ • ♥ • ♥ • ♥ • ♥ • ♥ • ♥ • ♥ • ♥ • ♥ • ♥ • ♥ • ♥

▶ Made On   ▶ Occasion

○ ....   ○ ....
○ ....   ○ ....
○ ....   ○ ....
○ ....   ○ ....
○ ....   ○ ....
○ ....   ○ ....
○ ....   ○ ....

♥ • ♥ • ♥ • ♥ • ♥ • ♥ • ♥ • ♥ • ♥ • ♥ • ♥ • ♥ • ♥ • ♥ • ♥ • ♥

 Notes

YamYam Recipe

Date ___ / ___ / 20 ___ DAY: . . . .

Name [..]

From the kitchen of [..]

Preparation Time [..........] Cooking Time [..........]

Ingredients

- ○ . . . .
- ○ . . . .
- ○ . . . .
- ○ . . . .
- ○ . . . .
- ○ . . . .
- ○ . . . .
- ○ . . . .
- ○ . . . .
- ○ . . . .

Directions

○ . . . .
. . . .
. . . .
. . . .
. . . .
. . . .
. . . .
. . . .
. . . .
. . . .
. . . .
. . . .
. . . .
. . . .
. . . .
. . . .

MAIN INGREDIENT

SEASONAL VARIATION

DIFFICULTY
- ☐ EASY
- ☐ MEDIUM
- ☐ HARD

COOKING TEMPERA-TUR

TOOLS TO USE

SERVES

DRINK PAIRING

Memories

Date First Tried: .... Date First Made: ....

This is: .... 's Favorite

▶ Made On   ▶ Occasion

○ .... ○ ....
○ .... ○ ....
○ .... ○ ....
○ .... ○ ....
○ .... ○ ....
○ .... ○ ....
○ .... ○ ....

 Notes

YamYam Recipe

Date ___ / ___ / 20 ___ DAY: . . . .

Name ....

From the kitchen of ....

Preparation Time: .... Cooking Time: ....

Ingredients

o .... o ....
o .... o ....
o .... o ....
o .... o ....
o .... o ....

Directions

o ....
....
....
....
....
....
....
....
....
....
....
....
....
....
....
....
....
....

MAIN INGREDIENT

SEASONAL VARIATION

DIFFICULTY
- [ ] EASY
- [ ] MEDIUM
- [ ] HARD

COOKING TEMPERA-
TUR

TOOLS TO USE

SERVES

DRINK PAIRING

54

Memories

Date First Tried: .... Date First Made ....

This is: ....'s Favorite

▶ Made On   ▶ Occasion

○ .... ○ ....
○ .... ○ ....
○ .... ○ ....
○ .... ○ ....
○ .... ○ ....
○ .... ○ ....
○ .... ○ ....

 Notes

YamYam Recipe

Date ___ / ___ / 20 ___ DAY: . . . .

Name : ....

From the kitchen of : ....

Preparation Time: .... Cooking Time: ....

Ingredients

- ○ ....
- ○ ....
- ○ ....
- ○ ....
- ○ ....

- ○ ....
- ○ ....
- ○ ....
- ○ ....
- ○ ....

Directions

○ ....
....
....
....
....
....
....
....
....
....
....
....
....
....
....
....

MAIN INGREDIENT

SEASONAL VARIATION

DIFFICULTY
- ☐ EASY
- ☐ MEDIUM
- ☐ HARD

COOKING TEMPERATUR

TOOLS TO USE

SERVES

DRINK PAIRING

♥ Memories

Date First Tried: ....   Date First Made: ....

This is: .... 's Favorite

♥•♥•♥•♥•♥•♥•♥•♥•♥•♥•♥•♥•♥•♥•♥•♥•♥

▶ Made On   ▶ Occasion

○ ....   ○ ....
○ ....   ○ ....
○ ....   ○ ....
○ ....   ○ ....
○ ....   ○ ....
○ ....   ○ ....
○ ....   ○ ....

♥•♥•♥•♥•♥•♥•♥•♥•♥•♥•♥•♥•♥•♥•♥•♥•♥

 Notes

Yam Yam Recipe

Date ___ / ___ / 20 ___ DAY: . . . .

Name ....

From the kitchen of ....

Preparation Time: .... Cooking Time: ....

Ingredients

○ . . . .   ○ . . . .
○ . . . .   ○ . . . .
○ . . . .   ○ . . . .
○ . . . .   ○ . . . .
○ . . . .   ○ . . . .

Directions

○ . . . .
. . . .
. . . .
. . . .
. . . .
. . . .
. . . .
. . . .
. . . .
. . . .
. . . .
. . . .
. . . .
. . . .

MAIN INGREDIENT

SEASONAL VARIATION

DIFFICULTY
☐ EASY
☐ MEDIUM
☐ HARD

COOKING TEMPERA-TUR

TOOLS TO USE

SERVES

DRINK PAIRING

58

Memories

Date First Tried: .... Date First Made: ....

This is: .... 's Favorite

▶ Made On

- ○ ....
- ○ ....
- ○ ....
- ○ ....
- ○ ....
- ○ ....
- ○ ....

▶ Occasion

- ○ ....
- ○ ....
- ○ ....
- ○ ....
- ○ ....
- ○ ....
- ○ ....

 Notes

YamYam Recipe

Date ___ / ___ / 20 ___ DAY: . . . .

Name : ....
From the kitchen of : ....

Preparation Time: .... Cooking Time: ....

Ingredients

- o ....
- o ....
- o ....
- o ....
- o ....

- o ....
- o ....
- o ....
- o ....
- o ....

Directions

- o ....
....
....
....
....
....
....
....
....
....
....
....
....
....
....
....
....
....

MAIN INGREDIENT

SEASONAL VARIATION

DIFFICULTY
- [ ] EASY
- [ ] MEDIUM
- [ ] HARD

COOKING TEMPERA-TUR

TOOLS TO USE

SERVES

DRINK PAIRING

Memories

Date First Tried: .... Date First Made: ....

This is: .... 's Favorite

▶ Made On ▶ Occasion

○ .... ○ ....

○ .... ○ ....

○ .... ○ ....

○ .... ○ ....

○ .... ○ ....

○ .... ○ ....

○ .... ○ ....

 Notes

YamYam Recipe

Date ___ / ___ / 20 ___ DAY: . . . .

Name : ....

From the kitchen of : ....

Preparation Time: .... Cooking Time: ....

Ingredients

- o ....
- o ....
- o ....
- o ....
- o ....

- o ....
- o ....
- o ....
- o ....
- o ....

Directions

- o ....
....
....
....
....
....
....
....
....
....
....
....
....
....
....
....

MAIN INGREDIENT

SEASONAL VARIATION

DIFFICULTY
- [ ] EASY
- [ ] MEDIUM
- [ ] HARD

COOKING TEMPERA-TUR

TOOLS TO USE

SERVES

DRINK PAIRING

62

Memories

Date First Tried :............:   Date First Made :............:

This is :..: 's Favorite

♥ • ♥ • ♥ • ♥ • ♥ • ♥ • ♥ • ♥ • ♥ • ♥ • ♥ • ♥ • ♥ • ♥

▶ Made On   ▶ Occasion

- ○ ....   ○ ....
- ○ ....   ○ ....
- ○ ....   ○ ....
- ○ ....   ○ ....
- ○ ....   ○ ....
- ○ ....   ○ ....
- ○ ....   ○ ....

♥ • ♥ • ♥ • ♥ • ♥ • ♥ • ♥ • ♥ • ♥ • ♥ • ♥ • ♥ • ♥ • ♥

 Notes

63

YamYam Recipe

Date ___ / ___ / 20 ___ DAY: . . . .

Name : ....

From the kitchen of : ....

Preparation Time : .... Cooking Time : ....

Ingredients

- ○ ....
- ○ ....
- ○ ....
- ○ ....
- ○ ....

- ○ ....
- ○ ....
- ○ ....
- ○ ....
- ○ ....

Directions

- ○ ....
- ....
- ....
- ....
- ....
- ....
- ....
- ....
- ....
- ....
- ....
- ....
- ....
- ....
- ....
- ....

MAIN INGREDIENT

SEASONAL VARIATION

DIFFICULTY
- ☐ EASY
- ☐ MEDIUM
- ☐ HARD

COOKING TEMPERA-TUR

TOOLS TO USE

SERVES

DRINK PAIRING

64

Memories

Date First Tried: .... Date First Made: ....

This is :...: 's Favorite

▶ Made On

▶ Occasion

○ ....
○ ....
○ ....
○ ....
○ ....
○ ....
○ ....

○ ....
○ ....
○ ....
○ ....
○ ....
○ ....
○ ....

 Notes

YamYam Recipe

Date ___ / ___ / 20 ___ DAY: . . . .

Name :..

From the kitchen of :..

Preparation Time :............ Cooking Time :............

Ingredients

- o ....
- o ....
- o ....
- o ....
- o ....

- o ....
- o ....
- o ....
- o ....
- o ....

Directions

- o ....
....
....
....
....
....
....
....
....
....
....
....
....
....
....
....
....
....

MAIN INGREDIENT

SEASONAL VARIATION

DIFFICULTY
- [ ] EASY
- [ ] MEDIUM
- [ ] HARD

COOKING TEMPERA-TUR

TOOLS TO USE

SERVES

DRINK PAIRING

66

Memories

Date First Tried: .... Date First Made: ....

This is: .... 's Favorite

▶ Made On

▶ Occasion

- ....
- ....
- ....
- ....
- ....
- ....
- ....

 Notes

YamYam Recipe

Date ___ / ___ / 20 ___ DAY: . . . .

Name : ....

From the kitchen of : ....

Preparation Time: .... Cooking Time: ....

Ingredients

o ....   o ....
o ....   o ....
o ....   o ....
o ....   o ....
o ....   o ....

Directions

o ....
....
....
....
....
....
....
....
....
....
....
....
....
....
....
....
....

MAIN INGREDIENT

SEASONAL VARIATION

DIFFICULTY
☐ EASY
☐ MEDIUM
☐ HARD

COOKING TEMPERA-TUR

TOOLS TO USE

SERVES

DRINK PAIRING

68

Memories

Date First Tried: .... Date First Made: ....

This is: .... 's Favorite

▶ Made On ▶ Occasion

○ .... ○ ....
○ .... ○ ....
○ .... ○ ....
○ .... ○ ....
○ .... ○ ....
○ .... ○ ....
○ .... ○ ....

 Notes

YamYam Recipe

Date ___ / ___ / 20 ___ DAY: . . . .

Name : ....

From the kitchen of : ....

Preparation Time : .... Cooking Time : ....

Ingredients

- ....
- ....
- ....
- ....
- ....

- ....
- ....
- ....
- ....
- ....

Directions

- ....
....
....
....
....
....
....
....
....
....
....
....
....
....
....
....
....
....

MAIN INGREDIENT

SEASONAL VARIATION

DIFFICULTY
- [ ] EASY
- [ ] MEDIUM
- [ ] HARD

COOKING TEMPERATUR

TOOLS TO USE

SERVES

DRINK PAIRING

Memories

Date First Tried: .... Date First Made: ....

This is: ....'s Favorite

▶ Made On

▶ Occasion

- ○ ....
- ○ ....
- ○ ....
- ○ ....
- ○ ....
- ○ ....
- ○ ....

- ○ ....
- ○ ....
- ○ ....
- ○ ....
- ○ ....
- ○ ....
- ○ ....

 Notes

YamYam Recipe

Date ___ / ___ / 20 ___ DAY: . . . .

Name ....

From the kitchen of ....

Preparation Time: .... Cooking Time: ....

Ingredients

- ○ ....
- ○ ....
- ○ ....
- ○ ....
- ○ ....

- ○ ....
- ○ ....
- ○ ....
- ○ ....
- ○ ....

Directions

- ○ ....
....
....
....
....
....
....
....
....
....
....
....
....
....
....
....
....
....
....

MAIN INGREDIENT

SEASONAL VARIATION

DIFFICULTY
- [ ] EASY
- [ ] MEDIUM
- [ ] HARD

COOKING TEMPERA-TUR

TOOLS TO USE

SERVES

DRINK PAIRING

72

Memories

Date First Tried: .... Date First Made ....

This is: .... 's Favorite

▶ Made On

▶ Occasion

○ ....
○ ....
○ ....
○ ....
○ ....
○ ....
○ ....

○ ....
○ ....
○ ....
○ ....
○ ....
○ ....

 Notes

YamYam Recipe

Date ___ / ___ / 20 ___ DAY: . . . .

Name: ....

From the kitchen of: ....

Preparation Time: .... Cooking Time: ....

Ingredients

- ....
- ....
- ....
- ....
- ....

- ....
- ....
- ....
- ....
- ....

Directions

- ....
- ....
- ....
- ....
- ....
- ....
- ....
- ....
- ....
- ....
- ....
- ....
- ....
- ....
- ....
- ....
- ....

MAIN INGREDIENT

SEASONAL VARIATION

DIFFICULTY
- [ ] EASY
- [ ] MEDIUM
- [ ] HARD

COOKING TEMPERATUR

TOOLS TO USE

SERVES

DRINK PAIRING

74

♥ Memories

Date First Tried: .... Date First Made : ....

This is : .... 's Favorite

♥♥♥♥♥♥♥♥♥♥♥♥♥♥♥♥♥♥

▶ Made On   ▶ Occasion

○ ....   ○ ....

○ ....   ○ ....

○ ....   ○ ....

○ ....   ○ ....

○ ....   ○ ....

○ ....   ○ ....

○ ....   ○ ....

♥♥♥♥♥♥♥♥♥♥♥♥♥♥♥♥♥♥

 Notes

YamYam Recipe

Date ___ / ___ / 20 ___ DAY: . . . .

Name ....

From the kitchen of ....

Preparation Time .... Cooking Time ....

Ingredients

- ....
- ....
- ....
- ....
- ....

Directions

- ....
....
....
....
....
....
....
....
....
....
....
....
....
....
....
....

MAIN INGREDIENT

SEASONAL VARIATION

DIFFICULTY
- [ ] EASY
- [ ] MEDIUM
- [ ] HARD

COOKING TEMPERATUR

TOOLS TO USE

SERVES

DRINK PAIRING

♥ Memories

Date First Tried .... Date First Made ....

This is .... 's Favorite

♥•♥•♥•♥•♥•♥•♥•♥•♥•♥•♥•♥•♥•♥•♥•♥

▶ Made On   ▶ Occasion

○ ....   ○ ....

○ ....   ○ ....

○ ....   ○ ....

○ ....   ○ ....

○ ....   ○ ....

○ ....   ○ ....

○ ....   ○ ....

♥•♥•♥•♥•♥•♥•♥•♥•♥•♥•♥•♥•♥•♥•♥•♥

 Notes

YamYam Recipe

Date ___ / ___ / 20 ___   DAY: . . . .

Name : ....

From the kitchen of : ....

Preparation Time : .... Cooking Time : ....

Ingredients

○ ....   ○ ....
○ ....   ○ ....
○ ....   ○ ....
○ ....   ○ ....
○ ....   ○ ....

Directions

○ ....
....
....
....
....
....
....
....
....
....
....
....
....
....
....
....

MAIN INGREDIENT

SEASONAL VARIATION

DIFFICULTY
☐ EASY
☐ MEDIUM
☐ HARD

COOKING TEMPERA-TUR

TOOLS TO USE

SERVES

DRINK PAIRING

78

Memories

Date First Tried: .... Date First Made : ....

This is : ....'s Favorite

▶ Made On   ▶ Occasion

○ ....   ○ ....
○ ....   ○ ....
○ ....   ○ ....
○ ....   ○ ....
○ ....   ○ ....
○ ....   ○ ....
○ ....   ○ ....

 Notes

YamYam Recipe

Date ___ / ___ / 20 ___ DAY: . . . .

Name : ....

From the kitchen of : ....

Preparation Time: .... Cooking Time: ....

Ingredients

- ○ ....
- ○ ....
- ○ ....
- ○ ....
- ○ ....

- ○ ....
- ○ ....
- ○ ....
- ○ ....
- ○ ....

Directions

- ○ ....
....
....
....
....
....
....
....
....
....
....
....
....
....
....
....
....

MAIN INGREDIENT

SEASONAL VARIATION

DIFFICULTY
- [ ] EASY
- [ ] MEDIUM
- [ ] HARD

COOKING TEMPERA-TUR

TOOLS TO USE

SERVES

DRINK PAIRING

Memories

Date First Tried: .... Date First Made : ....

This is :... 's Favorite

▶ Made On

▶ Occasion

- ○ ....
- ○ ....
- ○ ....
- ○ ....
- ○ ....
- ○ ....
- ○ ....

- ○ ....
- ○ ....
- ○ ....
- ○ ....
- ○ ....
- ○ ....
- ○ ....

 Notes

YamYam Recipe

Date ___ / ___ / 20 ___ DAY: . . . .

Name: ....

From the kitchen of: ....

Preparation Time: .... Cooking Time: ....

Ingredients

○ . . . . ○ . . . .
○ . . . . ○ . . . .
○ . . . . ○ . . . .
○ . . . . ○ . . . .
○ . . . . ○ . . . .

Directions

○ . . . .
. . . .
. . . .
. . . .
. . . .
. . . .
. . . .
. . . .
. . . .
. . . .
. . . .
. . . .
. . . .
. . . .
. . . .
. . . .

MAIN INGREDIENT

SEASONAL VARIATION

DIFFICULTY
☐ EASY
☐ MEDIUM
☐ HARD

COOKING TEMPERA-TUR

TOOLS TO USE

SERVES

DRINK PAIRING

82

Memories

Date First Tried: .... Date First Made :..................

This is :..:'s Favorite

▶ Made On   ▶ Occasion

o ....   o ....
o ....   o ....
o ....   o ....
o ....   o ....
o ....   o ....
o ....   o ....
o ....   o ....

 Notes

In large states public education will always be mediocre for the same reason that in large kitchens the cooking is usually bad

Friedrich Nietzsche

The Journey Continues

YamYam Recipe

Date ___ / ___ / 20 ___ DAY: . . . .

Name : ....

From the kitchen of : ....

Preparation Time :............: Cooking Time :............:

Ingredients

- o ....
- o ....
- o ....
- o ....
- o ....

- o ....
- o ....
- o ....
- o ....
- o ....

Directions

- o ....
....
....
....
....
....
....
....
....
....
....
....
....
....
....

MAIN INGREDIENT

SEASONAL VARIATION

DIFFICULTY
- [ ] EASY
- [ ] MEDIUM
- [ ] HARD

COOKING TEMPERATUR

TOOLS TO USE

SERVES

DRINK PAIRING

Memories

Date First Tried :............... Date First Made :...............

This is :..'s Favorite

▶ Made On   ▶ Occasion

○ ....   ○ ....
○ ....   ○ ....
○ ....   ○ ....
○ ....   ○ ....
○ ....   ○ ....
○ ....   ○ ....
○ ....   ○ ....

 Notes

YamYam Recipe

Date ___ / ___ / 20 ___ DAY: . . . .

Name ....

From the kitchen of ....

Preparation Time .... Cooking Time ....

Ingredients

o ....   o ....
o ....   o ....
o ....   o ....
o ....   o ....
o ....   o ....

Directions

o ....
....
....
....
....
....
....
....
....
....
....
....
....
....
....
....

MAIN INGREDIENT

SEASONAL VARIATION

DIFFICULTY
☐ EASY
☐ MEDIUM
☐ HARD

COOKING TEMPERA-TUR

TOOLS TO USE

SERVES

DRINK PAIRING

88

Memories

Date First Tried: .... Date First Made ....

This is .... 's Favorite

▶ Made On   ▶ Occasion

○ ....   ○ ....
○ ....   ○ ....
○ ....   ○ ....
○ ....   ○ ....
○ ....   ○ ....
○ ....   ○ ....
○ ....   ○ ....

 Notes

89

YamYam Recipe

Date ___ / ___ / 20 ___ DAY: . . . .

Name : ....

From the kitchen of : ....

Preparation Time : .... Cooking Time : ....

Ingredients

○ ....   ○ ....
○ ....   ○ ....
○ ....   ○ ....
○ ....   ○ ....
○ ....   ○ ....

Directions

○ ....
....
....
....
....
....
....
....
....
....
....
....
....
....
....
....

MAIN INGREDIENT

SEASONAL VARIATION

DIFFICULTY
- [ ] EASY
- [ ] MEDIUM
- [ ] HARD

COOKING TEMPERATUR

TOOLS TO USE

SERVES

DRINK PAIRING

Memories

Date First Tried :.............:   Date First Made :..........:

This is :............................:'s Favorite

▶ Made On   ▶ Occasion

○ ....   ○ ....
○ ....   ○ ....
○ ....   ○ ....
○ ....   ○ ....
○ ....   ○ ....
○ ....   ○ ....
○ ....   ○ ....

 Notes

YamYam Recipe

Date ___ / ___ / 20 ___ DAY: . . . .

Name :..

From the kitchen of :..

Preparation Time :..........: Cooking Time :..........:

Ingredients

○ .... ○ ....
○ .... ○ ....
○ .... ○ ....
○ .... ○ ....
○ .... ○ ....

Directions

○ ....
....
....
....
....
....
....
....
....
....
....
....
....
....
....
....

MAIN INGREDIENT

SEASONAL VARIATION

DIFFICULTY
☐ EASY
☐ MEDIUM
☐ HARD

COOKING TEMPERA-TUR

TOOLS TO USE

SERVES

DRINK PAIRING

92

Memories

Date First Tried: .... Date First Made ....

This is: .... 's Favorite

▶ Made On   ▶ Occasion

o ....   o ....
o ....   o ....
o ....   o ....
o ....   o ....
o ....   o ....
o ....   o ....
o ....   o ....

 Notes

YamYam Recipe

Date ___ / ___ / 20 ___ DAY: . . . .

Name : ....

From the kitchen of : ....

Preparation Time : .... Cooking Time : ....

Ingredients

- o ....
- o ....
- o ....
- o ....
- o ....

- o ....
- o ....
- o ....
- o ....
- o ....

Directions

- o ....
....
....
....
....
....
....
....
....
....
....
....
....
....
....

MAIN INGREDIENT

SEASONAL VARIATION

DIFFICULTY
☐ EASY
☐ MEDIUM
☐ HARD

COOKING TEMPERA-
TUR

TOOLS TO USE

SERVES

DRINK PAIRING

94

Memories

Date First Tried :............: Date First Made :............:

This is :....................................:'s Favorite

▶ Made On   ▶ Occasion

- ○ ....
- ○ ....
- ○ ....
- ○ ....
- ○ ....
- ○ ....
- ○ ....

 Notes

YamYam Recipe

Date ___ / ___ / 20 ___ DAY: . . . .

Name: ....

From the kitchen of: ....

Preparation Time: .... Cooking Time: ....

Ingredients

- ○ ....
- ○ ....
- ○ ....
- ○ ....
- ○ ....

- ○ ....
- ○ ....
- ○ ....
- ○ ....
- ○ ....

Directions

- ○ ....
- ....
- ....
- ....
- ....
- ....
- ....
- ....
- ....
- ....
- ....
- ....
- ....
- ....

MAIN INGREDIENT

SEASONAL VARIATION

DIFFICULTY
- ☐ EASY
- ☐ MEDIUM
- ☐ HARD

COOKING TEMPERATUR

TOOLS TO USE

SERVES

DRINK PAIRING

♥ Memories

Date First Tried: .... Date First Made: ....

This is: .... 's Favorite

▶ Made On ▶ Occasion

o .... o ....
o .... o ....
o .... o ....
o .... o ....
o .... o ....
o .... o ....
o .... o ....

 Notes

YamYam Recipe

Date ___ / ___ / 20 ___ DAY: . . . .

Name [................................]

From the kitchen of [................................]

Preparation Time [............] Cooking Time [............]

Ingredients

- o . . . .
- o . . . .
- o . . . .
- o . . . .
- o . . . .

- o . . . .
- o . . . .
- o . . . .
- o . . . .
- o . . . .

Directions

- o . . . .

MAIN INGREDIENT

SEASONAL VARIATION

DIFFICULTY
- [ ] EASY
- [ ] MEDIUM
- [ ] HARD

COOKING TEMPERA-TUR

TOOLS TO USE

SERVES

DRINK PAIRING

Memories

Date First Tried: .... Date First Made: ....

This is: .... 's Favorite

▶ Made On

o ....

o ....

o ....

o ....

o ....

o ....

o ....

▶ Occasion

o ....

o ....

o ....

o ....

o ....

o ....

o ....

 Notes

YamYam Recipe

Date ___ / ___ / 20 ___ DAY: . . . .

Name :...

From the kitchen of :...

Preparation Time :.........: Cooking Time :.........:

Ingredients

o .... o ....
o .... o ....
o .... o ....
o .... o ....
o .... o ....

Directions

o ....
....
....
....
....
....
....
....
....
....
....
....
....
....
....
....

MAIN INGREDIENT

SEASONAL VARIATION

DIFFICULTY
☐ EASY
☐ MEDIUM
☐ HARD

COOKING TEMPERA-TUR

TOOLS TO USE

SERVES

DRINK PAIRING

100

Memories

Date First Tried: .... Date First Made: ....

This is: ....'s Favorite

▶ Made On

▶ Occasion

○ .... ○ ....

○ .... ○ ....

○ .... ○ ....

○ .... ○ ....

○ .... ○ ....

○ .... ○ ....

○ .... ○ ....

 Notes

YamYam Recipe

Date ___ / ___ / 20 ___ DAY: . . . .

Name : ....

From the kitchen of : ....

Preparation Time :.............: Cooking Time :............:

Ingredients

- ○ ....
- ○ ....
- ○ ....
- ○ ....
- ○ ....

- ○ ....
- ○ ....
- ○ ....
- ○ ....
- ○ ....

Directions

- ○ ....
....
....
....
....
....
....
....
....
....
....
....
....
....
....
....

MAIN INGREDIENT

SEASONAL VARIATION

DIFFICULTY
- ☐ EASY
- ☐ MEDIUM
- ☐ HARD

COOKING TEMPERATUR

TOOLS TO USE

SERVES

DRINK PAIRING

Memories

Date First Tried: .... Date First Made ....

This is: .... 's Favorite

▶ Made On

- ○ ....
- ○ ....
- ○ ....
- ○ ....
- ○ ....
- ○ ....
- ○ ....

▶ Occasion

- ○ ....
- ○ ....
- ○ ....
- ○ ....
- ○ ....
- ○ ....

 Notes

Yam Yam Recipe

Date ___ / ___ / 20 ___ DAY: . . . .

Name: ....

From the kitchen of: ....

Preparation Time: .... Cooking Time: ....

Ingredients

- ○ ....
- ○ ....
- ○ ....
- ○ ....
- ○ ....
- ○ ....
- ○ ....
- ○ ....
- ○ ....
- ○ ....

Directions

- ○ ....
....
....
....
....
....
....
....
....
....
....
....
....
....
....
....
....

MAIN INGREDIENT

SEASONAL VARIATION

DIFFICULTY
- ☐ EASY
- ☐ MEDIUM
- ☐ HARD

COOKING TEMPERATUR

TOOLS TO USE

SERVES

DRINK PAIRING

104

Memories

Date First Tried: .... Date First Made ....

This is .... 's Favorite

▶ Made On

▶ Occasion

○ .... ○ ....
○ .... ○ ....
○ .... ○ ....
○ .... ○ ....
○ .... ○ ....
○ .... ○ ....
○ .... ○ ....

 Notes

YamYam Recipe

Date ___ / ___ / 20 ___ DAY: . . . .

Name: ....

From the kitchen of: ....

Preparation Time: .... Cooking Time: ....

Ingredients

- ....
- ....
- ....
- ....
- ....

- ....
- ....
- ....
- ....
- ....

Directions

- ....
....
....
....
....
....
....
....
....
....
....
....
....
....
....

MAIN INGREDIENT

SEASONAL VARIATION

DIFFICULTY
- [ ] EASY
- [ ] MEDIUM
- [ ] HARD

COOKING TEMPERATUR

TOOLS TO USE

SERVES

DRINK PAIRING

Memories

Date First Tried :............: Date First Made :............:

This is :..: 's Favorite

▶ Made On   ▶ Occasion

○ ....   ○ ....
○ ....   ○ ....
○ ....   ○ ....
○ ....   ○ ....
○ ....   ○ ....
○ ....   ○ ....
○ ....   ○ ....

 Notes

107

YamYam Recipe

Date ___ / ___ / 20 ___ DAY: . . . .

Name : ....

From the kitchen of : ....

Preparation Time : .... Cooking Time : ....

Ingredients

- ○ ....
- ○ ....
- ○ ....
- ○ ....
- ○ ....

- ○ ....
- ○ ....
- ○ ....
- ○ ....
- ○ ....

Directions

- ○ ....
- ....
- ....
- ....
- ....
- ....
- ....
- ....
- ....
- ....
- ....
- ....
- ....
- ....
- ....
- ....

MAIN INGREDIENT

SEASONAL VARIATION

DIFFICULTY
- [ ] EASY
- [ ] MEDIUM
- [ ] HARD

COOKING TEMPERATUR

TOOLS TO USE

SERVES

DRINK PAIRING

Memories

Date First Tried: .... Date First Made ....

This is: .... 's Favorite

▶ Made On   ▶ Occasion

○ ....   ○ ....
○ ....   ○ ....
○ ....   ○ ....
○ ....   ○ ....
○ ....   ○ ....
○ ....   ○ ....
○ ....   ○ ....

 Notes

109

YamYam Recipe

Date ___ / ___ / 20 ___ DAY: . . . .

Name : ....

From the kitchen of : ....

Preparation Time : .... Cooking Time : ....

Ingredients

- ○ ....
- ○ ....
- ○ ....
- ○ ....
- ○ ....

- ○ ....
- ○ ....
- ○ ....
- ○ ....
- ○ ....

Directions

- ○ ....
- ....
- ....
- ....
- ....
- ....
- ....
- ....
- ....
- ....
- ....
- ....
- ....
- ....
- ....
- ....
- ....

MAIN INGREDIENT

SEASONAL VARIATION

DIFFICULTY
- ☐ EASY
- ☐ MEDIUM
- ☐ HARD

COOKING TEMPERA-TUR

TOOLS TO USE

SERVES

DRINK PAIRING

Memories

Date First Tried: .... Date First Made: ....

This is: .... 's Favorite

▶ Made On

▶ Occasion

○ ....
○ ....
○ ....
○ ....
○ ....
○ ....
○ ....

○ ....
○ ....
○ ....
○ ....
○ ....
○ ....

 Notes

YamYam Recipe

Name : ....

From the kitchen of : ....

Preparation Time : .... Cooking Time : ....

Ingredients

- o ....
- o ....
- o ....
- o ....
- o ....

- o ....
- o ....
- o ....
- o ....
- o ....

Directions

- o ....
- ....
- ....
- ....
- ....
- ....
- ....
- ....
- ....
- ....
- ....
- ....
- ....
- ....
- ....
- ....

MAIN INGREDIENT

SEASONAL VARIATION

DIFFICULTY
- [ ] EASY
- [ ] MEDIUM
- [ ] HARD

COOKING TEMPERA-TUR

TOOLS TO USE

SERVES

DRINK PAIRING

♥ Memories

Date First Tried: .... Date First Made ....

This is: .... 's Favorite

▶ Made On   ▶ Occasion

- ○ ....   ○ ....
- ○ ....   ○ ....
- ○ ....   ○ ....
- ○ ....   ○ ....
- ○ ....   ○ ....
- ○ ....   ○ ....
- ○ ....   ○ ....

 Notes

YamYam Recipe

Date ___ / ___ / 20 ___ DAY: . . . .

Name :..

From the kitchen of :..

Preparation Time :............: Cooking Time :............:

Ingredients

- ○ ....
- ○ ....
- ○ ....
- ○ ....
- ○ ....

- ○ ....
- ○ ....
- ○ ....
- ○ ....
- ○ ....

Directions

- ○ ....
- ....
- ....
- ....
- ....
- ....
- ....
- ....
- ....
- ....
- ....
- ....
- ....
- ....
- ....
- ....

MAIN INGREDIENT

SEASONAL VARIATION

DIFFICULTY
- ☐ EASY
- ☐ MEDIUM
- ☐ HARD

COOKING TEMPERA-TUR

TOOLS TO USE

SERVES

DRINK PAIRING

♥ Memories

Date First Tried: .... Date First Made ....

This is: .... 's Favorite

▶ Made On   ▶ Occasion

○ ....   ○ ....
○ ....   ○ ....
○ ....   ○ ....
○ ....   ○ ....
○ ....   ○ ....
○ ....   ○ ....
○ ....   ○ ....

 Notes

Yam Yam Recipe

Date ___ / ___ / 20 ___ DAY: . . . .

Name : ....

From the kitchen of : ....

Preparation Time : .... Cooking Time : ....

Ingredients

○ ....
○ ....
○ ....
○ ....
○ ....

○ ....
○ ....
○ ....
○ ....
○ ....

Directions

○ ....
....
....
....
....
....
....
....
....
....
....
....
....
....
....
....
....

MAIN INGREDIENT

SEASONAL VARIATION

DIFFICULTY
☐ EASY
☐ MEDIUM
☐ HARD

COOKING TEMPERA-TUR

TOOLS TO USE

SERVES

DRINK PAIRING

Memories

Date First Tried: .... Date First Made ....

This is ....'s Favorite

▶ Made On   ▶ Occasion

○ ....   ○ ....
○ ....   ○ ....
○ ....   ○ ....
○ ....   ○ ....
○ ....   ○ ....
○ ....   ○ ....
○ ....   ○ ....

 Notes

YamYam Recipe

Date ___ / ___ / 20 ___ DAY: . . . .

Name ....

From the kitchen of ....

Preparation Time: .... Cooking Time: ....

Ingredients

- ○ ....
- ○ ....
- ○ ....
- ○ ....
- ○ ....

- ○ ....
- ○ ....
- ○ ....
- ○ ....
- ○ ....

Directions

- ○ ....
....
....
....
....
....
....
....
....
....
....
....
....
....
....
....
....

MAIN INGREDIENT

SEASONAL VARIATION

DIFFICULTY
- [ ] EASY
- [ ] MEDIUM
- [ ] HARD

COOKING TEMPERA-TUR

TOOLS TO USE

SERVES

DRINK PAIRING

118

Memories

Date First Tried: .... Date First Made ....

This is ....'s Favorite

▶ Made On   ▶ Occasion

○ ....   ○ ....
○ ....   ○ ....
○ ....   ○ ....
○ ....   ○ ....
○ ....   ○ ....
○ ....   ○ ....
○ ....   ○ ....

 Notes

119

YamYam Recipe

Date ___ / ___ / 20 ___ DAY: . . . .

Name: ....

From the kitchen of: ....

Preparation Time: .... Cooking Time: ....

Ingredients

- ○ ....
- ○ ....
- ○ ....
- ○ ....
- ○ ....

- ○ ....
- ○ ....
- ○ ....
- ○ ....
- ○ ....

Directions

- ○ ....
....
....
....
....
....
....
....
....
....
....
....
....
....
....
....
....
....

MAIN INGREDIENT

SEASONAL VARIATION

DIFFICULTY
- ☐ EASY
- ☐ MEDIUM
- ☐ HARD

COOKING TEMPERA-TUR

TOOLS TO USE

SERVES

DRINK PAIRING

120

Memories

Date First Tried: .... Date First Made: ....

This is: ....'s Favorite

▶ Made On   ▶ Occasion

- ○ ....   ○ ....
- ○ ....   ○ ....
- ○ ....   ○ ....
- ○ ....   ○ ....
- ○ ....   ○ ....
- ○ ....   ○ ....
- ○ ....   ○ ....

 Notes

121

YamYam Recipe

Date ___ / ___ / 20 ___ DAY: . . . .

Name ....

From the kitchen of ....

Preparation Time: .... Cooking Time: ....

Ingredients

- ○ ....
- ○ ....
- ○ ....
- ○ ....
- ○ ....

- ○ ....
- ○ ....
- ○ ....
- ○ ....
- ○ ....

Directions

- ○ ....
....
....
....
....
....
....
....
....
....
....
....
....
....
....

MAIN INGREDIENT

SEASONAL VARIATION

DIFFICULTY
- ☐ EASY
- ☐ MEDIUM
- ☐ HARD

COOKING TEMPERA-TUR

TOOLS TO USE

SERVES

DRINK PAIRING

122

Memories

Date First Tried: .... Date First Made ....

This is ....'s Favorite

▶ Made On   ▶ Occasion

- ○ .... ○ ....
- ○ .... ○ ....
- ○ .... ○ ....
- ○ .... ○ ....
- ○ .... ○ ....
- ○ .... ○ ....
- ○ .... ○ ....

 Notes

YumYum Recipe

Date ___ / ___ / 20 ___ DAY: . . . .

Name:

From the kitchen of:

Preparation Time: . . . . Cooking Time: . . . .

Ingredients

- . . . .
- . . . .
- . . . .
- . . . .
- . . . .

- . . . .
- . . . .
- . . . .
- . . . .
- . . . .

Directions

- . . . .
. . . .
. . . .
. . . .
. . . .
. . . .
. . . .
. . . .
. . . .
. . . .
. . . .
. . . .
. . . .
. . . .
. . . .

MAIN INGREDIENT

SEASONAL VARIATION

DIFFICULTY
- [ ] EASY
- [ ] MEDIUM
- [ ] HARD

COOKING TEMPERA-TUR

TOOLS TO USE

SERVES

DRINK PAIRING

124

Memories

Date First Tried: .... Date First Made ....

This is :...:'s Favorite

▶ Made On   ▶ Occasion

○ ....   ○ ....
○ ....   ○ ....
○ ....   ○ ....
○ ....   ○ ....
○ ....   ○ ....
○ ....   ○ ....
○ ....   ○ ....

 Notes

YamYam Recipe

Date ___ / ___ / 20 ___ DAY: . . . .

Name :...

From the kitchen of :...

Preparation Time :.............: Cooking Time :...........:

Ingredients

- ○ ....
- ○ ....
- ○ ....
- ○ ....
- ○ ....

- ○ ....
- ○ ....
- ○ ....
- ○ ....
- ○ ....

Directions

○ ....
....
....
....
....
....
....
....
....
....
....
....
....
....
....
....

MAIN INGREDIENT

SEASONAL VARIATION

DIFFICULTY
☐ EASY
☐ MEDIUM
☐ HARD

COOKING TEMPERA-TUR

TOOLS TO USE

SERVES

DRINK PAIRING

126

Memories

Date First Tried :................: Date First Made :................:

This is :..: 's Favorite

▶ Made On

○ ....
○ ....
○ ....
○ ....
○ ....
○ ....
○ ....

▶ Occasion

○ ....
○ ....
○ ....
○ ....
○ ....
○ ....
○ ....

 Notes

YamYam Recipe

Date ___ / ___ / 20 ___ DAY: . . . .

Name :...:

From the kitchen of :...:

Preparation Time :..........: Cooking Time :..........:

Ingredients

- ○ ....
- ○ ....
- ○ ....
- ○ ....
- ○ ....

- ○ ....
- ○ ....
- ○ ....
- ○ ....
- ○ ....

Directions

- ○ ....
....
....
....
....
....
....
....
....
....
....
....
....
....
....
....
....

MAIN INGREDIENT

SEASONAL VARIATION

DIFFICULTY
- [ ] EASY
- [ ] MEDIUM
- [ ] HARD

COOKING TEMPERA-TUR

TOOLS TO USE

SERVES

DRINK PAIRING

Memories

Date First Tried: .... Date First Made ....

This is ....'s Favorite

▶ Made On   ▶ Occasion

○ ....   ○ ....
○ ....   ○ ....
○ ....   ○ ....
○ ....   ○ ....
○ ....   ○ ....
○ ....   ○ ....
○ ....   ○ ....

 Notes

YamYam Recipe

Date ___ / ___ / 20 ___ DAY: . . . .

Name :..:

From the kitchen of :..................................:

Preparation Time :..........: Cooking Time :..........:

Ingredients

- o ....
- o ....
- o ....
- o ....
- o ....

- o ....
- o ....
- o ....
- o ....
- o ....

Directions

- o ....
  ....
  ....
  ....
  ....
  ....
  ....
  ....
  ....
  ....
  ....
  ....
  ....
  ....
  ....
  ....
  ....
  ....

MAIN INGREDIENT

SEASONAL VARIATION

DIFFICULTY
- [ ] EASY
- [ ] MEDIUM
- [ ] HARD

COOKING TEMPERA-TUR

TOOLS TO USE

SERVES

DRINK PAIRING

130

Memories

Date First Tried :..................: Date First Made :..................:

This is :..: 's Favorite

▶ Made On

- ○ ....
- ○ ....
- ○ ....
- ○ ....
- ○ ....
- ○ ....
- ○ ....

▶ Occasion

- ○ ....
- ○ ....
- ○ ....
- ○ ....
- ○ ....
- ○ ....
- ○ ....

 Notes

Yam Yam Recipe

Date ___ / ___ / 20 ___ DAY: . . . .

Name : ....

From the kitchen of : ....

Preparation Time : .... Cooking Time : ....

Ingredients

o ....
o ....
o ....
o ....
o ....

o ....
o ....
o ....
o ....
o ....

Directions

o ....
....
....
....
....
....
....
....
....
....
....
....
....
....
....
....

MAIN INGREDIENT

SEASONAL VARIATION

DIFFICULTY
- [ ] EASY
- [ ] MEDIUM
- [ ] HARD

COOKING TEMPERATUR

TOOLS TO USE

SERVES

DRINK PAIRING

Memories

Date First Tried: .... Date First Made ....

This is: ....'s Favorite

▶ Made On   ▶ Occasion

○ ....   ○ ....

○ ....   ○ ....

○ ....   ○ ....

○ ....   ○ ....

○ ....   ○ ....

○ ....   ○ ....

○ ....   ○ ....

 Notes

YamYam Recipe

Date ___ / ___ / 20 ___ DAY: . . . .

Name : ....

From the kitchen of : ....

Preparation Time : .... Cooking Time : ....

Ingredients

- ○ ....
- ○ ....
- ○ ....
- ○ ....
- ○ ....

- ○ ....
- ○ ....
- ○ ....
- ○ ....
- ○ ....

Directions

- ○ ....
....
....
....
....
....
....
....
....
....
....
....
....
....
....
....
....

MAIN INGREDIENT

SEASONAL VARIATION

DIFFICULTY
- [ ] EASY
- [ ] MEDIUM
- [ ] HARD

COOKING TEMPERA-TUR

TOOLS TO USE

SERVES

DRINK PAIRING

Memories

Date First Tried: .... Date First Made ....

This is ....'s Favorite

▶ Made On

- ....
- ....
- ....
- ....
- ....
- ....
- ....

▶ Occasion

- ....
- ....
- ....
- ....
- ....
- ....
- ....

 Notes

Writing is just as natural to me as getting up and cooking breakfast

Friedrich Nietzsche

Name	Phone N°

Telephone List

Name	Phone N°

Name	Phone N°

Oven Temperature Conversion Chart: Fahrenheit, Celsius and Gas Mark

Fahrenheit	Celsius	Gas Mark	Terminology
275 degrees F	140 degrees C	1	Very Cool or Very Slow
300 degrees F	150 degrees C	2	Cool or Slow
325 degrees F	165 degrees C	3	Warm
350 degrees F	177 degrees C	4	Moderate
375 degrees F	190 degrees C	5	Moderate
400 degrees F	200 degrees C	6	Moderately Hot
425 degrees F	220 degrees C	7	Hot
450 degrees F	230 degrees C	8	Hot
475 degrees F	245 degrees C	9	Hot
500 degrees F	260 degrees C	10	Very Hot

Volume Conversions

Teaspoons	Tablespoons	Ounces	Cups	Pints	Quarts	Gallons	Milliliters	Liters
3	1	1/2	1/16				15	0.015
12	4	2	1/4				60	0.06
24	8	4	1/2				125	0.125
48	16	8	1	1/2	1/4	1/16	250	0.25
		16	2	1	1/2	1/8	500	0.5
		32	4	2	1	1/4	950	0.95
		128	16	8	4	1	3800	3.8

Without Cooking

There is nothing but
DARKNESS
&
CHAOS